Lost in the Storm

Written by Karl Newson

Illustrated by Michael Emmerson

... there lives a little fire dragon called Smokey.

Smokey is an adventurer.
She's a soarer and a swooper.
She's a super loop-the-looper!

But once upon a thunderstorm,
one night, not long ago,

while Smokey soared above a hill,

the winds began to blow.

Then the flashing lightning **struck!**
And the rumbling thunder **rolled!**

And in the cloud, so dark and grey,
Smokey turned and lost her way ...

... and plunged
into the sea —
into the stormy,
icy cold!

There, upon the sea,
she felt so frightened on her own.
The water crashed
and splished and splashed!

But Smokey **wasn't** alone.

A whale rose up
in the stormy waters,
appearing by her side.

And with a **whoosh**
it said to Smokey,
"Would you like a ride?"

"Yes, please!" Smokey shivered,
with a quiver in her speech.
"Thank you, kindly whale.
Could you take me to the beach?"

Smokey climbed aboard —
she wasn't frightened any more.
The whale told her stories
as they headed to the shore ...

... below a twinkling starry sky,
while the storm was chased away,
and the sun began to rise,
as the night became the day.

Smokey searched along the coast to find a way back home.

She couldn't see the mountain high.

Her wings were still too wet to fly.

The cliffs were far too tall to climb!

But something made her stop and listen, trickling in her ear.
"The river!" Smokey gasped —
and she knew that she was near.

But here, the river fell into
a tumbling waterfall,
where the valley met the cliffs –
with no way through at all.

Smokey felt like giving up,
but something made her look ...
between the rocks,
behind the fall.

She found a hidey-nook!

Then she saw a little light.
She smiled and she rejoiced!
"Hello, little dragon!"
said a small and friendly voice.

An island boy was drawing
on the wall inside the nook:

a forest and a river
and a dragon on the roam,
and an old and jagged mountain
Smokey recognised as home!

Smokey told the boy about
the thunder and the lightning:
how the flashes and the rumbles
made it all so very frightening,
how she fell into the sea, and how
a whale heard her call.

And the boy drew her adventure using chalk upon the wall ...

"Thunder," said the boy, "is just the sky singing a song."
"Lightning," said the boy, "is just the clouds singing along."

Smokey dried her wings beside the fire's warming glow.
Then the boy said, "Follow me — there's a secret way to go."

Through a twisting cave they went,
and out into the light!
Smokey thanked the island boy
and sprang up into flight.

Up above the river
and the valley and the hill,
she swooped towards the mountain high —
but then was frozen still.

Between her and the mountain
was a storm cloud up ahead!

Smokey felt the rain begin.
 She felt a worry creeping in.
  She felt her tummy start to spin.

But something made her think instead
of what the island boy had said.

Smokey closed her eyes.
She was afraid, but she was brave —
and she soared into the storm,
just like the drawing in the cave!

At the very pointy top
of an old and jagged mountain,

where a winding river flows
and a wild forest grows...

... a little fire-dragon **swooped** and landed in the rain.

And she looked back through the storm, with the biggest, proudest smile — and she could not wait to go adventuring again!

Published by Pearson Education Limited, 80 Strand, London, WC2R 0RL.

www.pearsonschools.co.uk

Text © Pearson Education Limited 2020

Written by Karl Newson

Project managed and edited by Just Content Limited

Original illustrations © Pearson Education Limited 2020

Illustrated by Michael Emmerson

Designed and typeset by Collaborate Agency Limited

This publication is protected by copyright, and permission should be obtained from the publisher prior to any prohibited reproduction, storage in a retrieval system, or transmission in any form or by any means, electronic, mechanical, photocopying, recording, or otherwise. For information regarding permissions, request forms and the appropriate contacts, please visit https://www.pearson.com/us/contact-us/permissions.html Pearson Education Limited Rights and Permissions Department.

Unless otherwise indicated herein, any third party trademarks that may appear in this work are the property of their respective owners and any references to third party trademarks, logos or other trade dress are for demonstrative or descriptive purposes only. Such references are not intended to imply any sponsorship, endorsement, authorisation, or promotion of Pearson Education Limited products by the owners of such marks, or any relationship between the owner and Pearson Education Limited or its affiliates, authors, licensees or distributors.

First published 2020

23 22 21 20

10 9 8 7 6 5 4 3 2 1

British Library Cataloguing in Publication Data

A catalogue record for this book is available from the British Library

ISBN 978 0 435 20145 6

Copyright notice

All rights reserved. No part of this publication may be reproduced in any form or by any means (including photocopying or storing it in any medium by electronic means and whether or not transiently or incidentally to some other use of this publication) without the written permission of the copyright owner, except in accordance with the provisions of the Copyright, Designs and Patents Act 1988 or under the terms of a licence issued by the Copyright Licensing Agency, Barnards Inn, 86 Fetter Lane, London EC4A 1EN (www.cla.co.uk). Applications for the copyright owner's written permission should be addressed to the publisher.

Printed in Slovakia by Neografia

Note from the publisher

Pearson has robust editorial processes, including answer and fact checks, to ensure the accuracy of the content in this publication, and every effort is made to ensure this publication is free of errors. We are, however, only human, and occasionally errors do occur. Pearson is not liable for any misunderstandings that arise as a result of errors in this publication, but it is our priority to ensure that the content is accurate. If you spot an error, please do contact us at resourcescorrections@pearson.com so we can make sure it is corrected.